T0128593

Tell Me Their Stories:

Amazing Women From A - Z

JENNIFER GRECCO

Archway Publishing books may be ordered through booksellers or by contacting:

Archway Publishing
1663 Liberty Drive
Bloomington, IN 47403
www.archwaypublishing.com
844.669.3957

Interior Image Credit: Corlette Douglas

ISBN: 978-1-4808-9910-0 (sc)
ISBN: 978-1-4808-9911-7 (e)

Print information available on the last page.

Archway Publishing rev. date: 03/09/2021

ARCHWAY
PUBLISHING

In Memory of Ruth Bader Ginsberg, the second woman to sit on the Supreme Court of the United States. Ruth said, "Women belong in all places where decisions are being made. It shouldn't be that women are the exception."

Ruth, you left fingerprints of courage and determination on our lives.

In Recognition of Kamala Harris' historic election and becoming the first woman, and person of color, Vice President of the United States. Kamala said, "What I want young women and girls to know is: You are powerful and your voice matters."

Kamala, you inspire us to see ourselves in new ways and to never stop dreaming big.

A is for Amelia Earhart

Who had the courage to fly
Across the ocean alone
She was brave way up high.

B is for **B**illy Jean King

Who had the confidence to dare
A man to play tennis
And won fair and square.

is for Cleopatra

Egypt's strong ruler B.C.
Who learned 12 languages
Math and astronomy.

D is for Diana Vreeland

Who liked wearing nice clothes
She helped dress Jackie Kennedy
And became the editor of *Vogue*.

E is for Eleanor Roosevelt

Who was President Roosevelt's wife
And stood up for others
Every day of her life.

F is for Frida Kahlo

Who was a painter by trade
And used bright bold colors
In the paintings she made.

G is for Gloria Steinem

Who stood up for girls
And showed them they had choices
Like boys in the world.

H is for Harriet Tubman

Who was determined and brave
And risked her life
For the hundreds she saved.

I is for Indira Gandhi

Who was a Prime Minister well known
For the courage and strength
She had always shown.

J is for Joan of Arc

A fearless warrior for sure
Who led the French Army
During the 100 Years War.

K is for Katherine Johnson

Who used math to guide
A spaceship to safety
And save the astronaut inside.

L is for Liz (Elizabeth) Blackwell

Who was the first woman to be
A doctor in the United States
Hard work was the key.

M is for Mae Jemison

The first African American astronaut who
Blasted off into space
In 1992.

N is for Nancy Pelosi

Who helped Congress decide
Which laws to pass
And which to let slide.

O is for Oprah Winfrey

Who was a talk-show host on TV
She was a voice for social justice
And equal opportunity.

P is for Patricia Bath

Who thought vision was a right
And discovered how to fix cataracts
To improve people's sight.

is for Queen Victoria

Who became queen at 18
And grew the British Empire
To the largest it had been.

R is for Rosa Parks

Who sat on a bus
She sat where she wanted
And caused quite a fuss.

s is for Sonia Sotomayor

The third woman to stand
Alongside the men
On the Supreme Court of our land.

T is for Sojourner Truth

Who stood up and fought
To win her son back
In a segregated court.

U is for Yoshiko Uchida

Who stayed hopeful and strong
Even though others believed
She did not belong.

V is for Vera Rubin

Who created quite the chatter
When through her telescope
She discovered dark matter.

W is for Williams

Serena and Venus too
Who have been tennis champions
Since 2002.

gave up her spot for you to see

There's still a place for your story.
(*Draw a self-portrait here!*)

Y is for Malala Yousafzai

Who fought for girls to be able
To attend school in Pakistan
And have a seat at the table.

z is for Zora Neale Hurston

Who won many a prize
For writing about the struggles
She saw with her eyes.

That ends the alphabet
from A to Z...
... You too can be
anything you want to be !

ABOUT THE AUTHOR

Jennifer Grecco graduated from Barnard College, an all-women's college in New York City. While there, she worked to empower young girls and change the gendered narrative to one of confidence, accomplishment, and inclusiveness. Jennifer now attends the University of Michigan Law School.

ABOUT THE ILLUSTRATOR

Corlette Douglas is an African American, New York-based illustrator. While pursuing her bachelor's in illustration at the Fashion Institute of Technology, she developed a passion for creating cute content for children's media from the perspective of a person of color. Learn more at https://corcorart.squarespace.com.

Printed in the United States
by Baker & Taylor Publisher Services